THE 10 BEST HARDSTYLE KICK TRICKS EVER

DISCOVER 10 ESSENTIAL TIPS HOW TO MAKE A HARDSTYLE KICK IN FL STUDIO, ABLETON, CUBASE OR LOGIC PRO

HARDSTYLE MUSIC KICK DRUM SOUND DESIGN FOR EDM PRODUCTION

BY CEP FROM SCREECH HOUSE

ISBN-13: 978-1713130475

ISBN-10: 1713130475

PREFACE

In this quick but exclusive booklet, you will discover the 10 best hardstyle kick tricks ever. These top 10 powerful strategies are carefully selected to help you make your hardstyle kick downright spectacular.

HOW TO MAKE A HARDSTYLE KICK

If you have ever tried making a powerful hardstyle kick, you probably already know that you need a chain of mixer effects with equalizers and distortions. After all, this is what everyone is always saying, right? Yet very frustratingly, this is where it usually ends. So, you have these questions: what do they mean by that? How should I use those effects so that I too can get that professional sound?

That's why in this special publication, we will go over 10 of the best hardstyle kick tricks that you can use immediately. By simply applying them, you may actually be surprised about the fast improvements you can make. Whether you're using FL Studio, Ableton, Pro Tools, Cubase or Logic Pro, these strategies will work with any software, with any app or with and plugins you wish to use.

Of course, this list is limited to 10 proven tricks that I personally found to be the most helpful. Also, make sure to read until the end, else you will miss any vital golden nuggets you may need to succeed.

MAKING A HARDSTYLE KICK

As a caveat upfront, following the advice herein doesn't mean you don't have to do the work anymore. Obviously, you still must practice and play around to make it happen. However, by knowing some proven strategies, it will easily cut your learning curve in half.

Speaking about cutting your learning curve in half, have you already downloaded my free hardstyle sample pack? It contains many ready-made high-quality files, including unique hardstyle kick samples. Just visit this link to start your download: https://screechhouse.com/free-hardstyle-sample-pack and come back to this booklet, as you don't want to miss any crucial tips I'm about to share.

THE DEFINITIVE PLATFORM FOR EDM PRODUCERS

So, who am I? My nickname is Cep and you may know me from my other well-received books (https://screechhouse.com/books) and EDM community, called *Screech House. Screech House* has an appreciated YouTube channel (https://youtube.com/screechhouse) and website (https://screechhouse.com) that you can visit by visiting these links. While you're at it, also feel free to subscribe to *Screech House* on YouTube to receive very rare EDM production content in your feed.

Furthermore, the short book you're reading now contains content that you can find as an article on my website and as a video on YouTube. So, if you want visuals, I invite you to visit by following these links:

➢ **Website:** https://screechhouse.com/the-10-best-hardstyle-kick-tricks-ever

➢ **YouTube:** https://youtu.be/F7ELZJpNB7Y

Although these resources are completely free, by owning this booklet, you actually support my work. For the price of your evening dinner, you make it possible for me to make content like this. So, thank you for that. But above all, having an eBook or paperback laying in your house looks way more legitimate. Nobody is impressed by a YouTube video or webpage anymore, but everybody thinks you're legit when you show them a book.

Now, as for demonstration purposes, you can find an FL Studio hardstyle kick tail in the video mentioned above. Again, visit the links. The tail is the part where you shape the hardstyle kick and give it its characteristics. It's also the most difficult element to make, so let's focus on making it awesome. Mind you though, it's not yet a complete hardstyle kick but serves as a great example for today's list.

Before we begin, please understand that you're reading a very brief booklet. The information is condensed into a fast but intense summary to get the points across quickly. Why? Because most people prefer shorter books and "to the point" material. This comes with the digital age and shorter attention spans. So, keep your focus as long as it lasts, because many crucial tips will fly by one after the other at lightning speed.

However, if you do find yourself having the desire to get more depth with a certain topic, don't feel tempted to give a one-star rating, but simply join my YouTube channel and website. You can most likely find an answer there, but if that fails, just leave a comment immediately below a video lesson. If you do that and if I'm able to provide a suitable answer, your suggestion will very likely be transformed into a new video and/or article. So, don't hesitate to ask your questions in the comments section when you have one.

Now, take some popcorn and let's start with number 10 on our list of the best hardstyle kick tricks.

"The quality of our music is a direct reflection of our level of understanding."

CONTENTS

"Applied knowledge gives you the experience to become successful."

HARDSTYLE KICK TRICK #10:

START WITH A PUNCHY SINE OR TRIANGLE WAVEFORM

Before you can build your hardstyle kick, you need to have an audio signal to work with. Typically, people advice you to use a 909 kickdrum sample or drum machine. This is very solid advice, but it works just as well when you start with a plain old sine or triangle wave. You can find a sine or triangle wave on basically any synthesizer out there. Just look on the oscillator's section where you can select the right waveform.

Based on personal taste, give your sine or triangle a quick pitch-drop at the start of the sound, using the pitch envelope. This will produce a punch that brings the kick into existence.

Of course, don't forget to play a note to produce an actual audio signal. Thereby, shoot for a note at a fundamental frequency in the sub bass area. This is usually somewhere between E3 and A#3 (or E2 and A#2). It's best to pick a note that is in line with the root note of your melody. This ensures your kick plays in harmony with it.

ESSENTIAL MUSIC THEORY BASICS

Now, when you want to learn more about notes and essential music-theory basics, simply go get The Ultimate Melody Guide (https://screechhouse.com/books/the-ultimate-melody-guide). Just visit the link and you can start right now.

Lastly, make sure to send your instrument to the mixer where you can add a bunch of effects to transform it into a massive hardstyle kick. Let's find out how…

HARDSTYLE KICK TRICK #9:

USE MULTIPLE EQUALIZERS AND DISTORTIONS

To stay true to the common advice out there, yes, you DO want to use multiple equalizers and distortions to create a hardstyle kick. Thereby, you typically want to alternate them alongside other effects. More on that later but in short, putting an equalizer before a distortion shapes the signal the distortion has to work with. This results in unique sounds which gives you ultimate control over your hardstyle kick-building process.

As a point of attention though, you typically want to "EQ" and "distort" more aggressively in the beginning of your effects chain and more subtle towards the end. Else, if you overdo it, you may destroy the crunchy quality of the kick. And that's not something we want.

HARDSTYLE KICK TRICK #8:

USE AN EQUALIZER WITH A 20 HZ LOWCUT AS A FIRST EFFECT

Now here is a neat little trick you may want to try out. Add an equalizer as your very first effect and give it a steep lowcut (or high pass) around 20 Hz. You probably won't hear the difference immediately, but once you start adding other effects, especially distortions, you will notice that it's easier to make your kick sound right. This has to do with the way the distortion affects the signal after it's being lowcut.

If you have never tried it, just give it a shot and let's see if you too can reap the benefits. Talking about benefits, you will still get 7 more highly effective tactics, so grab another bowl of popcorn and let's continue.

HARDSTYLE KICK TRICK #7:

USE BIPOLAR CLIP DISTORTIONS

No, we don't mean the mental condition here, but the quote-on-quote "special" way a distortion processes the audio signal. By using the bipolar option on a clip distortion plugin, if it allows for it, you can treat both poles of a waveform separately. This is called "asymmetric" distortion and it enables you to get unique distortion shapes and sounds. But above all, using the bipolar function is a quick way to add harmonic-rich content to your emerging hardstyle kick. These so-called "harmonics" is just an array of musical frequencies your hardstyle kick needs to sound right. Of course, depending on how YOU want it to sound.

Mind you though, when you apply bipolar distortion, the waveform can move away from its center. After all, if one pole differs from the other, the balance of the sound is likely to shift toward one or the other. This may result in volume loss or loss of power. To get your kick back in center, you can try using an equalizer with a lowcut around 20 to 40 Hz and/or boost it with a unipolar distortion, which is just a fancy way of saying: a normal distortion.

One last trick; with some of the distortion plugins, especially later in your chain, apply a certain mix level and don't distort the whole signal. This produces added characteristics yet doesn't affect the entire kick. Inevitably, too much distortion will ruin your results. So, watch out.

HARDSTYLE KICK TRICK #6:

USE EQUALIZERS TO ADD A BUNCH OF MID FREQUENCIES

Here's one tip you've probably already heard many times before: add a bunch of mid frequencies with an equalizer. The mid frequencies are essential for the characteristics of a hardstyle kick. But it's also important to do it right. Else, your kick may end up too hollow or too shallow.

So, how do you do it right? Well, it depends on many variables, but here are some guidelines that may work for you:

➢ Add the mid frequencies quite early in your mixer effects chain. Preferably right after the first distortion.

➢ Then, aim somewhere between 400 to 900 Hz, depending on your preferences.

➢ Also, add a good amount of around 12 to 24 db. Thereby, use a bell curve on your equalizer and play around with the steepness of the band. A wide band fills the whole kick with a wider arrange of mid frequencies, while a narrow band produces a punchier type of emphasis.

Now, adding mid frequencies will boost the kick in this range of the spectrum. Thus, to bring back some balance, you may want to reduce the mid frequencies a little bit later in your effects chain. Another way of restoring the balance is by simply boosting the lower and higher frequencies, which we will talk about very soon. So, stay tuned.

HARDSTYLE KICK TRICK #5:

USE EQUALIZERS TO MAKE LOW CUTS

We already briefly touched the subject at number 8 on this list but making low cuts can work wonders for your hardstyle kicks. When you add a steep low cut with an equalizer you create some room before the signal enters a distortion. As low frequencies tend to brick up the sound, you allow it to open up by removing them, resulting in interesting distortion shapes, added harmonics and even a heavier type of sound.

As a general advice, try to shoot for a steep lowcut anywhere from 20 Hz up until may be 60 Hz. Personally, I found the 30 to 40 Hz range work the best. Thereby, use this trick with a couple of different equalizers throughout your chain of effects, especially the first few in your effects chain. However, near the end, it's usually best to be more careful. Else, you may ruin your hardstyle kick a little bit by getting flat and kind of a plastic sounding.

Please be aware that you may want to add in some extra lower frequencies further in your chain to make up for any lost ones here. The lower frequencies can be boosted with a so-called "low shelf" band on an equalizer anywhere from 40 to 200 Hz. Of course, depending on what and how much you want to add. Don't overdo it though, as it might crush your kick.

HARDSTYLE KICK TRICK #4:

USE EQUALIZERS TO ADD SOME

HIGHER FREQUENCIES

High frequencies are important. They provide well-needed freshness and clarity. In a way, having plenty of higher frequencies boost the perceived quality. On top of that, adding them will also restore the frequency balance of the sound, especially after amplifying the mid frequencies.

That's why it's very fruitful to use your equalizers to include a bunch of higher frequencies. Thereby, you have to use your ears to hear how much your kick actually needs. Don't be afraid to experiment. Just play around with a so-called "high shelf" band on an equalizer and center it anywhere around 1500 Hz all the way up to around 12000 Hz. Hell, even 800 Hz can produce outstanding results.

As for everything, you can be more aggressive with your approach in the beginning and usually more subtle towards the end.

Since we're also near the end of this list, we are now entering the top 3. So, refill that bowl with popcorn one last time and let's start with number 3.

HARDSTYLE KICK TRICK #3:

ADD SOME REVERB

Have you ever tried using a reverb in your hardstyle kick effects chain? If so, that's awesome. You see, reverb functions in a way that it gives your kick a sense of space and serves as a fusion tool. Also, it can create a nice stereo effect. But above all, it can produce extra crunchiness, power and pressure, depending on how you use it. And that in particular is what we want for our hardstyle kick.

Now, there are many different reverb plugins "out there", each having their own flavor and effect on the sound. Therefore, simply pick your favorite reverb plugin and experiment with its settings. What you want to pay attention to is the room size and decay time. It can work well to select a small to medium room and to use a relatively short decay time. For example, 0.5 seconds or anything like that.

As a word of caution: don't drown your kick in reverb by giving it a too high "wet" level. Similarly, don't dry your kick out with a too low "wet" level. Usually, a medium amount, let's say between 30% and 60% is about right. This is quite different from the amount of reverb you typically use for hardstyle leads, as I advise in the Supersaw FL Studio instruction guide (https://screechhouse.com/books/supersaw-fl-studio). Again, visit the link to start immediately.

Finally, you may want to experiment with including two or even three reverbs in your chain, whereas the first one can easily be added as the third or fourth effect.

HARDSTYLE KICK TRICK #2:

CREATE A FILTER SWEEP

I already dedicated an entire tutorial on this topic, that you can easily access by visiting this link: https://screechhouse.com/elements-hardstyle-kick-fl-studio. But in short, a filter sweep will make your hardstyle kick more dynamic. It adds extra bark and bounce, which in a way can sound heavier. Furthermore, when you use it correctly, a filter sweep adds an array of moving mid frequencies, that essentially gives it a slightly more professional feel.

In order to create a filter sweep, you want to use a filter plugin that contains a cutoff envelope. Alternatively, and for the more advanced individuals, automate a peaking band of an equalizer with an automation clip. But let's stick with the cutoff envelope on a filter.

With a cutoff envelope you can tell the filter how to move its frequency band. Thereby, you will probably want to use a bandpass filter type (BP for short), as it produces a band of amplified frequencies that you can use to create the sweep. Furthermore, shoot for a starting frequency around 400 to 900 Hz by setting that as a cutoff value.

To determine the cutoff envelope duration, it's a good idea to set it to one beat. One beat aligns with the natural length of your hardstyle kick.

To prevent an overload of mid frequencies and a too dominant sweep, it's probably not a good idea to use a fully wet signal. Aim for a mix level of around 40% to 60%. This way, around 40% to 60% of your signal will be affected by the filter. You can achieve that by enabling two filters and only activate one. The other one simply takes up 50% of the signal that will not be processed, thus passing through unmodified.

Of course, there are many more filter options you can use that you can benefit from. That's why you have to keep experimenting and don't be afraid to go wild.

START WITH THE BASICS FIRST

Nonetheless, if you're having troubles following this, don't worry. Start with the basics fist. That's why you can now obtain the Sound Design for Beginners guide (https://screechhouse.com/books/sound-design-for-beginners) which takes you along all the essential synthesizer settings you simply must know to achieve high-quality sound design, including envelopes and filters. Just visit the link to get started right away.

And now it's time to reveal the number 1 spot…

HARDSTYLE KICK TRICK #1:

PAY ATTENTION TO THE ORDER

OF EFFECTS

You may think this is a weird pick as my number one tip, but when you understand it deeply, a hardstyle kick usually follows a proven pattern, also tailored to your own way of working. There's a logical structure where the order and type of effects play a massive role. In other words, when do you use which effect? That's the question. And this is not chosen randomly. Although, some random picks here and there can absolutely produce surprising results.

Now, what you want to develop is the intuition of knowing which effect should be used in a given moment or situation. This is hard to teach, but luckily quite easy to learn. All you need is some time where you practice and experience with the conviction that you are going to succeed.

Moreover, absorb quote-on-quote "good" information that has proven to work. If you model that, you raise your chances of success tremendously, as I talk about in my book: The Success Mindset for Music Production (https://screechhouse.com/books/the-success-mindset-for-music-production).

6 EFFECTIVE HARDSTYLE KICK TIPS

But to give you some practical tips, here are 6 logical guidelines that have proven to work for me. So, maybe you can take advantage of that as well.

1. Always use an equalizer after and/or before a distortion to shape the way the next distortion must respond, depending on what you'd like to hear next.

2. Use an equalizer early in the chain to add mid frequencies, create a steep lowcut and add some higher frequencies. This will immediately set the foundation for the hardstyle kick.

3. Create a filter sweep after the first reverb.

4. Use a reverb after the equalizer that contains the added mid frequencies.

5. Only make minor changes with subtle equalization and distortion at the final stage of the effects chain.

6. Always end with a clip distortion to prevent the signal to shoot above the 0-decibel limit, which is the maximum loudness for digital audio.

Now, there are many more "rules" you can use, but at some point, it's doing you more harm than good. You have to come to your own conclusions about what to do in certain situations, which, like it or not, is always different, yet is never truly random. So, don't take anything literally and keep your mind open. You must develop your own experience and way of working. Ultimately, the sound of your final hardstyle kick is what matters, not necessarily how you got there.

And again, all these tips apply to the TAIL part of the kick, which is often the hardest part to produce. Once your tail is finished, you can save it as a sample. The sample can then be used in a new layering project where you add a sub bass and create the tok or punch.

Now, those are topics for another day, but if you want all these types of samples ready for use, just visit this link to download my free hardstyle sample pack right now: https://screechhouse.com/free-hardstyle-sample-pack.

ARE YOU A BEGINNER? START HERE...

Lastly, if you're still having difficulties piecing the music production puzzle together, don't worry. We're all at a different level. So, if you're relatively new and you need more help to break through the beginner's phase quickly, you can easily start by reading my well-received books. Just visit the links below and find out what they have to offer to you. Thereby, you can read the first 10% of each book for free to discover exactly which benefits you'll get.

READ NOW

- ➢ The Ultimate Melody Guide:
  https://screechhouse.com/books/the-ultimate-melody-guide

- ➢ Sound Design for Beginners:
  https://screechhouse.com/books/sound-design-for-beginners

- ➢ Supersaw FL Studio:
  https://screechhouse.com/books/supersaw-fl-studio

- ➢ The Success Mindset for Music Production:
  https://screechhouse.com/books/the-success-mindset-for-music-production

➢ FL Studio Beginner's Guide:

https://screechhouse.com/books/fl-studio-beginners-guide

I'd love to teach you more in my other books and don't forget to join my YouTube channel (https://youtube.com/screechhouse) and website (https://screechhouse.com) by visiting these links.

See you there!

- Cep

(Music producer, author & creator of *Screech House*)

GET YOUR FREE SAMPLE PACK

To help you kickstart your music productions, I've created a free EDM sample pack to share with you. Visit the link below to start your download.

https://screechhouse.com/free-hardstyle-sample-pack

www.ingramcontent.com/pod-product-compliance
Lightning Source LLC
Chambersburg PA
CBHW070905070326
40690CB00009B/2002